ON SUNDAY AFTERNOONS

poems by

Richard Becker

Finishing Line Press
Georgetown, Kentucky

ON SUNDAY AFTERNOONS

Copyright © 2022 by Richard Becker
ISBN 978-1-64662-828-5 First Edition
All rights reserved under International and Pan-American Copyright Conventions. No part of this book may be reproduced in any manner whatsoever without written permission from the publisher, except in the case of brief quotations embodied in critical articles and reviews.

ACKNOWLEDGMENTS

Grateful thanks and acknowledgement is given to the following for publishing individual poems:

"Equinox" and "Evocation" in *America*
"Chesapeake" in *The Baltimore Review*
"Holding On To The Light" in *Bottomfish*
"Driving to Santa Fe" and "Lagoon On The James" in *Columbia*
Cantos I, VII and VIII from *Fates*, a chapbook of *The Literary Review*
"Sonos Locus: Newfane, Vermont" and "A Cape Cod Evening" in *Main Street Rag*
"Shekhinah" in *Poetica*
"Letter from the Super 8" in *Slipstream*
"Prospect Park," Crossing Newburgh Bridge," Visit, "Archimedes," "Park Slope" and "On Sunday Afternoons" in *U City Review*.

Publisher: Leah Huete de Maines
Editor: Christen Kincaid
Cover Art: David from D Lobos Photography
Author Photo: Doris Wylee-Becker
Cover Design: Elizabeth Maines McCleavy

Order online: www.finishinglinepress.com
also available on amazon.com

Author inquiries and mail orders:
Finishing Line Press
PO Box 1626
Georgetown, Kentucky 40324
USA

Table of Contents

Equinox 1

Lagoon on the James 2

Driving to Santa Fe 3

Prospect Park 4

Sweet Gum 5

Archimedes 6

Chesapeake 7

Crossing Newburgh Bridge 8

Visit 10

Sonos Locus: Newfane, Vermont 13

Shekhinah 15

Letter from the Super 8 16

On Sunday Afternoons: 17

Park Slope 19

A Cape Cod Evening 22

"Reclining Figure" 23

Soliloquy 24

from *Fates*

    I. An almost naked freight-yard whore 25

    VII. In this park and graveyard 26

    VIII. It's night. Eyes closed. And I withdraw 31

Evocation 34

Autumn 35

Equinox

A squadron of blackbirds rests
on my oak tree. Their rustling and chatter
remind me of those ominous winds before a spring storm.

I bang a broom against the trunk and send them flocking
shudder at their lengthening festoon across the sky

that gathers in a whirlpool on the horizon
pours through an invisible funnel
and is gone.

Lagoon on the James

Cloaked in leafage, a cat-eyed
crescent inhales bottom spoon-fry
with each playful thrust.
                                    Heron sport him
in the shallows that lap
against shoal rock, like young girls' babble
on a quick nights' porch. One strikes him through,
easing the wriggling load lengthwise,
smoothing its passage with mezzo-lingual

jolts. Far cry from home,
and a boathouse away,
fishermen suck six packs and piss on the wall
dreaming of diamonds found in a pickerel. Lonely men
put out in pick-ups empty-handed at day's end,
hearts and fish heads pinned
on snap-swiveled stringers.

At night frogs blurt thick sauced sounds.
A lagoon sized white haired beast rises
in their growl, is stabbed to pieces
by moon stalks. Ooze bubbles up in its milky wake
to feed the river slugs.
                                    Leopard gar unload a year's
length ribboned fog in cloak of fatherhood
that populates gar cradles
with gar fry.

Driving to Santa Fe

I hitch a ride with a Vegas show girl.
While she drives we play lap-top chess.
A storm withdraws from its wet skin.
Her driving glides the mesas
on the big board in the big room,

no dice thrown. A nice doe rides
across the shadow of a butte looming tall and
traveling on its own steam. She calls her pawns
to do-si-do, en passant beneath the clearing sky.
My king allemandes a two-step with his rook.

We speed past roadside armadillo carcasses
with bloated cracking skin. Buzzards arch
like bishops swooping down diagonals, tally
dead, suspicious of our hundred horses. Any
flesh they find they grab in their quick talons.

Stopping at a vista point, we look,
we breathe, we see pink masonry
and drink the air like vino Sangioveto.
Night animals' voices rise cantabile falsetto
in mock solemnity. She cranes her neck,

her pretty silhouette, as if to cipher poetry
from the skies' faint flicker. I fear
the portent of her mood and whistle
for her return. I work my thumb
inside her palm and we drive on.

Prospect Park

You strained not to squint in sun
having swallowed tears when scolded
for the grass stains on your dress.

Breezes trembling the distant sounds
of bagpipes from Army Arch
dusted your cheek with auburn hair

and skittered dried oak leaves past
my feet off camera. And in your lap
Mrs. Hershey's coal black spaniel

made you smile at the shutter click
that when in wake of yawning caught
its tongue in its lip. Mom called it

red felt sewn on. And it's the only
color not yet faded after all this time.

Sweet Gum

Tired of raking seed balls
we felled the huge old tree.
But it shocked us when
we felt as if we'd killed
a sentient being. We were not
vegetarians. On Yom Kippur,
Papa passed a rooster[1] overhead
and sang, "I am for life but you,
you are for death." Atoning
also cleans the balance sheet
of wrongs done us and wrongs
we did: we forgive and beg
forgiveness, praying next will be
a good year *hashona tova.*

Long after crying when its wood
was hauled away, we still could not
forgive *ourselves*, a Rabbi's
daughters, for whom omnipresent
chainsaws in our neighborhood
kept on reigniting the remorse.
Remember you said taking
it down was "burial in reverse,"
"because," you said, "its soul
lives on in the felled tree's crater."

Last night after plucking a chicken
and draining its blood (God's
uncollected light), I traced
your imagined spirit's flight
out the window to the yard
and through the limbs of a gum
I planted for you there: whose
uncollected seed will stay
unraked for all my time *kinahora.*[2]

---

[1] https://www.chabad.org/library/article_cdo/aid/989585/jewish/Kaparot.htm
[2] a contraction of three Yiddish words: kayn ayin hara, literally "not (kayn) the evil (hara) eye (ayin).

Archimedes

Summer days pass like pages
through a press: a here today
and gone tomorrow river
of time that moves and stays.
Moves and stays. A Moon. A Sun.

A clock. The dump is full[3] of projects
in a heap or yet to be. Torch lamp.
Oval mirror. Garter belt. Half a table.
Ask the old man when he's not
o-ho-hoe-ing. When he's not

too busy tracking what you will
release as surely as his this or that.
And we. We watch the beauties
dropping from your arms and
strewn about the place

to howl and fade and spill
down drains as surely as each day
is caught in tree boughs for the night
as in an hour glass of sand.
We teach the young to pan

for dust of 19.32 specific gravity.[4]
No more. No less. Days of
summer sun go down. Go on.
Dross gone the glitter's here,
salvaged in autumn's alchemy.

---

[3] Wallace Stevens's "The Man on the Dump."
[4] 19.32 g/cm3 is the specific gravity of gold.

Chesapeake

Dying embers of sun on shore
blink from Yankee Point.
In forecastle still I face
your face asleep. Your eyelids flicker.

Dogs bark. Doves reply.
Many thoughts are one.
A million suns beneath
your skin in every pulse.

And as we sway a mast ticks
stars across the sky the way
a yad is held to cue each line
of parchment text,[5] right to left,

right to left. We sway on
rippling waves that rock
us into dreaming of the sea
on the sea that dreamt us.

---

[5] יָד is the Hebrew word, yad, for "hand." A yad is a hand-shaped pointer used in synagogue to chant Torah text.

Crossing Newburgh Bridge

> "...it was as if there were an invisible thread
> joining all the outside birds" —Elizabeth Bishop[6]

She knows Elizabeth Bishop went to Vassar.
And her rejection of her Mom's potpourri—once
a garnered keepsake—was not Earth
shattering but left me in dismay as she pressed
it in my palm when we parted just outside
the college on the Hudson River Walkway (re-
purposed long after the 1974 fire from what
in Bishop's day had been a railroad bridge).

An eclipse only dreamt of up till now dims
the morning sky over Poughkeepsie
as I head down I-84 for home. Ten miles
from the college is an abyss for missing her.
It's 9 a.m. and a large gray Moon cuts
across the Sun as she blurts, "Dammit Dad,
it's so unreal," on the car's Bluetooth.
And I whisper, "Yes I know. And daughter,
please be well. Be well." Merging with I-87
I stop at a Vista Point with other moon-
watchers, none of whom squeezes
potpourri in their pocket. Moon blocked Sun,
three words dispel preventing any 'pining
for absent daughter' clichés. The potpourri.
The bridge farewell. The abyss.
And nature's own eclipse.

Last century, on another continent French jets
hailed an eclipse that shut down Paris.
Everyone from parapet sitters to street flâneurs.
From café squatters to map-bound tourists.
Everyone donned safety glasses. All heads
tilted skyward. But cloudy skies cast a pall.

Nor did jets thrill me in those anti-nuke,
anti-war days when my thoughts rang

[6] *Vassar Journal of Undergraduate Studies* (May 1933).

quixotic as Picasso's in the Great War
with his bathos pitch to camouflage
French soldiers with harlequin diamonds.
In front of his museum on Rue de Thorigny
in mid-day night, a chanteuse cranking
a hurdy-gurdy sang to me, warbling how
her heart wept rain[7] —in vibrato voice
that from an age so sad and strange seemed
to brush my cheeks with French kisses.

Back here the mountain view comes alive
with flecks of light and I behold two worlds
in trinity with ours. The Sun whole
though dimmed by mountain fog.
The Moon, a shrunk white cloud. And
while I stand on this outcropping where
late summer heat waves rise off hoods
of remaining cars, I detect the intimate
scent of my ex-wife's sock drawer.

And the daughter of our long and troubled
marriage is off to college on whose
school breaks I must confront the changes
teachers and her reading will have made.

11 a.m. For all I know Bishop's
invisible thread that fixes overhead
a large flock of geese in vee-formation guides
the galaxies in space and holds the Earth
in place: its chemicals and ghosts.

---

[7] «Il pleure dans mon Coeur», Paul Verlaine.

Visit

My wife sleeps through
the dryer's clattering sound
that keeps me wide awake
thinking of my friend
the composer who has passed.

A modernist poet once
dubbed death the mother
of beauty. I don't fear it,
only its arrival and oblivion.

As he napped, neighbors' calves
lowed for milk and cows
for milking while we walked
in meadow grass without him.
And Carol warned not to forget
to check our feet for ticks.
She spoke not of the flowers
or the grass, thick and bright
as they were.
                Later when we ate
the homemade muffins
contemplating our life's joys
and sorrows, family and friends
we had or missed, I asserted
that I ranked Carol's muffins
high among life's joys
at which point he snarled,
"I'm afraid they just go
through me."
                Three months
later Carol's postcard came
in perfect hand telling
of his courage and of where
in nearby mountains
they would pour his ashes
now dissolved in ground
and loam and cow cakes
and on Catskill's orange
Canna lilies.

My view is
Mt. Washington would have hung
them longer in the air.
And while the illusion
of his essence swirls around
me like Freud's bees of the id
I begin to till the vessel
of his death's exigent birth
of "Beauty" urging
me toward things I do not know
and beyond those which
I used to think I did.

One of his enduring traits
was the gift of gallows humor
that got him and those
near him through the pain
and fear of death's oblivion.

And as we gathered for
goodbyes at the door
that afternoon in Willow
the cows again were lowing.
And we were hugging
when he quipped "O if only
you could lend me some
of your own body weight!"
Then during the long
drive home, we could yet
hope for his recovery
that was simply not to be.

Tonight in bed, my wife
and I recounted those two days
in Willow. At ten, we heard
the Amtrak rumble on the
north bank of the river.
And at eleven a pair of
great-horned owls plotted
bearings at the minor third.

"Busy" she said, "trapping
supper," and I said, "I
wouldn't want to be a vole
right now." And she replied
some minutes before sleep,
"Sounds point to a world
of constancy and change."

I go to the laundry room
and gaze at pants and shirts
and underthings drying
in the vortex that as a kid
I used to watch intently,
as kids do, when they thrust
and cling and fly apart.
But it's midnight now
and I switch the dryer off.

Sonos Locus: Newfane, Vermont

> *"The tree which moves some to tears of joy is
> in the eyes of others only a green thing simply
> in the way. But to the eyes of [persons] of
> imagination, nature is imagination."* —William Blake [8]

Not till it sank
behind the clouds
could a jet be heard,

in whose wake
local sounds would
soon regain their hold.

The wind-stirred trees,
invisible to some,
beautiful to others

& beautiful
for beauty's sake
to even more,

were to the rest
just green things
in the way.

A Carolina dove
framed morning gloom,
"too wit too woo
too wit too woo too."

Local plovers call-
and-answered
from the power poles

with their antecedes
and their consequents,
diving Doppler-bent

---

[8] William Blake letter, August 23, 1799.

like frog pond bee buzz
in the blooming lily pads.
And a man on the road

with pen and pad, seeing
his Mother's face
in tree crowns, wondered

why his poems
so strong one day
were weak the next,

when read in well-
considered light,
and, as he nears

the age of his Father
at death, if nature
were for him no less

imagination than
it was for them.

Shekhinah[9]

Whether in victory or defeat
with all the risks of war
                              not knowing why
or what it is or where
nothing redeems like coming home.

Li Po mistaking the moon-lit floor
for frost on the ground looks up

at the moon in the mountains
and thinks of home. [10]
                    A laboratory
test-bird bangs into cage bars
until freed.
            And at birth when life
breaks free
            to breathe the vital mortal air
though there be nothing there
                                    we want it still
feeling its presence not knowing why
or what it is or where.

---

[9] Rabbinically, God's presence in the world.
[10] My paraphrase of Chinese, T'ang Dynasty poet known also as Li Bai, 701–762.

Letter from a Super 8

I said, "I'm much too young,"
and you retorted that you liked your fruit hung high.

Remember how you once jangled the bracelet
I had left on your piano,

while holding it above your full head of hair
(thinning now to what I call distinguished

as in last July's New Music News)? Remember
shaking all the charms and how you teased

the girl, embarrassing the woman
when you called me in your deep baritone?

Had not your voice flushed
my face amid the noisy pony tails to burn

with shame and pride, I would not
have pinched myself with the clasp.

Drawing blood. Remember your concern, ten years ago?
As I write from a continent away

the same bracelet's tingling risks its strong, secret lure.
Risks its lure from this motel room

and a troubled marriage. I invoke the hamza hand,
a wishbone, and the evil eye

casting a spell on you to come fly down and taste
from this tree's low bough its ripe fruit.

On Sunday Afternoons

I do okay with a Capuchin monkey and a cashbox by my side:
a music teacher moonlighting on weekends at the corner
of seventh and second. Just across the street, my son wants
"Stars and Stripes" and "Sidewalks of New York," staples
of the hurdy-gurdy. Listening he will ride his truck around
the room before his nap.
                        On the roof his mother's taking down
the laundry under cold, January sun. A Piper Cub circling
over Lady Liberty, whose buzz reminds her of our vow not
to tell him how before we went to War, the U.S. blocked asylum
for passengers aboard the SS St. Louis.[11] Not after his school's
attempt to deny her run for president of the PTA, when they
found out she was Jewish.
                            She pockets clothespins in my jacket,
worn over her blue pinstripe housedress; folds and drops bed sheets
in a wicker basket rocking it on the hard uneven roof tar, where
Sam from 6-A sometimes lets him feed his pigeons.
                                              The brood
return from wherever pigeons go and now alight the roof rail, circle
his feet, and make for the coop. I see my wife's and his head bob
among the sheets. My son would hear their jovial chat were he not
sound asleep, though he's probably too young to know what might
be hiding in such smiles and laughter.
                                    He builds model ships and planes.
When he broke a destroyer's rigging, his tears surely tasted salty as
a Gowanus Bay offshore breeze. He dreams of planes and ships
and how his will save the world. "Peace through strength," headlines
the papers, the radio, and the new TV.
                                         In his dream he's on the deck
of a carrier. Its Thunder Jets start mixing with my wife's loud radio
tuned to "Ghost Riders in the Sky," the rounding up of the devil's herd:
Yippie yi yay! Yippie yi ooh! Ghost Riders in the Sky!
                                                      The radio's
"Magic Eye" vibrates Vaughn Monroe's bravado verse and smooth
crooned choruses. I gladly play for coins dropped in my corner cash box,
adding up to Chinese dinner down the street for the three of us.

---

[11] 1939 ship returned to Europe with mostly Jewish refugees of whom 254 were killed at Auschwitz and Buchenwald.

                                                                    Now
my son wakes up and gazes, squinting through sunlit dust wraiths
from his cot, not at dreamed of waves and Thunder Jets, or of the red-eyed
longhorns in the loud song that woke him, but at my black leather jacket
on a nail, and through the stair window above the laundry basket at no
gray city buildings. Just bright sky.

Park Slope

Blackouts end. Relit, bright city lights
are new to us. Soft as cat paws over snow,
headlights shine through sixth floor blinds
casting oblong beads of yellow light
on bedroom walls.
                    We call them Good
& Plenty for the candy at the Roxy's
Saturday cartoons between victory
newsreels Dad says preach to the choirs
of the Brooklyn Navy Yard that rebuilt
America's Fleet.
                 Not the candy's pink
and white or white and purple of the beads
Algonquins made from dead sea shells
on display at museums, our beads
are very much alive.
                   Their yellow neon
starting and stopping on the wall's a kind
of Martian code. To crack it as you know
we invent that micro-intertransitronómeter:
Train wire. Battery. Paper clips
and small light switch.
                        On the street Bay Ridge
trolleys have a voice all their own. Red hot
cinders pop from head to toe. From above
and below
                they spark and hiss like newly
evolved flame tongue dinosaurs. Both wheels
and catenary sparking and hissing all over
Brooklyn. Daily in the street we fire bullets
pointing index fingers
                       at the cars or trucks
whose backfire knocks black hats off
black horses in our own wild west
as in radio shootouts fought for
Truth and Justice
                 and The American Way:
bullets careening off rocks, whistling
with ricochet sound effects. Remember how

we root for Lone Ranger and for Tanto
neither of whom gets killed.
       Nor do they
ever kill the bad guy. But cello tremolos
shake us in my cowboy and your cowgirl
boots when in the settling dust we learn
our heroes thwarted evil doers,
         as Liberty
defeats the force of Tyranny. After school kaboom
kaboom! My cap gun in the living room!
Mom's and Dad's chairs are your palomino
and my stallion.
       Nightly we rub sparks from vinyl
head boards. And once when Jane, your best friend
dances in the bedroom, neon Good & Plenty
brightly stream across her chest
and necklace crucifix.
      Cellphones press
some ears as if in pain. Convening crows
squawk in the Park as I cross that's silent
but for homeless snoring. And still awake
some young couples stir
       in aubades by the pond.
Park lamps off. I can't believe it's decades
since we were like them. You with your first.
Me with I forget which. What with these
age spot hands
      and me in the old bedroom down
the street from the park where now a fancy
B&B abuts the church. I pry loose floorboards
for old stashes of caps and (Remember?)
the illicit ladyfingers!
      A penlight from
my faculty emeritus briefcase sees me
through a child's eye: pressing rosette
coronas from my palm as if from dough
with a cookie cutter. We behold the rush
of blood and oxygen. Was that us?
Then and now? I cannot wait for dusk to glint

the "poor" and "huddled masses" carved
in Liberty. All the headlights
                              coming up
soft as cat paws over snow. Were you here
you'd see our Good & Plenty on the wall
stop and start. Red light. Green light.

School kid driving uncle's wired car.
Private Eye shadowing a yellow cab.
A young woman's rushed to hospital
in labor at 3:00 a.m. And I wait again
for completion of the endless change
of night to day when Good & Plenty's
just a darkened theater's candy treat.

"A Cape Cod Evening" [12]

Summer's over and the tourists are gone
leaving mostly owners
on the Cape.

There's a woman in a dress, standing
next to a man in a tee shirt
seated on

the back doorstep of a white Cape Cod.
He's about to toss their collie dog
a stick, but she spies me

and may come greeting any moment.
Their gaze is so fixed on her
they don't see me

here, off canvas, past their
backyard's tall, brown
switchgrass.

---

[12] Edward Hopper's "Cape Cod Evening"

"Reclining Figure" [13]

It is easy to miss the sculpting of Henry Moore:

The roundnesses of his bodies, the hollowed out
richnesses where a lifetime can dwell for generations.

Remembered: still and warm inside. No perturbation
or woe despite perturbation and woe all around.

The silences received drift deeper in the eyes of viewers
now called patrons and deeper in their psyches

than can come from any book. Deeper because
imagined: where the truth is found the way we find it

filling infinitely round silence or infinitely round
space in any given time or place.

---

[13] https://www.vmfa.museum/piction/6027262-8070571/

Soliloquy

I was afraid when Grampa died
and Mama said, "Death is sleep."
I squeezed my eyes shut. Faking.
Praying, *Don't sleep! Don't sleep.*

Then Dad at the light switch, allayed
my fear, prompting me by crooning,
"Lights out! Lights out!" a fun
routine that put me right to sleep.

Older now, I pray to Sleep with Keats's
hymn. Life today's a dream I write—
a boat I till, for my time. And my dream's
a type of death denial not too far

removed from pulpit claims of risen flesh
albeit not so young and beautiful. One day
I'll show you the soliloquies he read.
But you should know, for him, 'nothing's

good or bad but thinking makes it so,'
meant his father's ghost made madness
faked or real and its dream of just revenge
inform yet pollute young Hamlet's mind

with what being was, and his dream
become the nightmare of ten deaths all
the realer with four eyewitnesses: king's
ghost, audience, onstage players, and…

Wait! Dad, is that you in the aisle seat?
Cap-à-pie[14] in sharkskin, voice so hoarse and
touch, so cold and out of reach? Don't go!

---

[14] head to foot, *Hamlet, I.2.200*, [Hor. to Ham., of Ghost] "a figure like your father, / Armed at point exactly cap-à-pie."

Fates [15]

I.

An almost naked freight-yard whore
whose work begins when the night shift ends
rubs her back on a tall lamp pole,
leans and smokes, then spins half round,
one leg coiling while the other clamps the ground.

Now purring and in long slow strides, she
sidles over to an iron fence, throws her head
back so lamplight shimmers on her G-string's
rhinestones and begins. Clasping a fence finial
she moans and to boom box music thrusts

her hips as groaning switchers couple
in the dark. Letting go, she flamencos
on stilettos, clapping hands above her head:
"Ay! Ay!" Then cupping and un-cupping
her imposing breasts she shimmies amid

groans of yardmen, who swing lanterns
that could pass for fiery heads, as they grope
the rusted spear points for her touch.

---

[15] Clotho spins life's thread. Lachesis measures the thread. Atropos cuts the thread.

VII.

> *"And as to you Life I reckon you are the leavings of many deaths,*
> *No doubt I have died myself ten thousand times before."*
> — Song of Myself, Canto 49, Walt Whitman.

In this park and graveyard, silt
from the last flood dons
the feet of lichened trees.

And my anxious memory points me
toward you, toward your garden
and piazza. Look, there's the parasol.

Late spring's spinning maple seeds.
Whirligigs we called them,
and they're coming down like crazy.

We recount the term he taught us first,
"Dicotyledons," then, "Dicots,"
to reinforce and ease. And now

you stick one on my nose,
dubbing it "nose hood," a new term
you long since have learned

from myth—medieval, I surmise
and quip, "No Lenny, these are not

for race cars!" We always will be
Brooklynites. Washed up
on the shoals of the Gowanus.

For us there's no metropolis.
Our Park Slope's but a tiny speck
compared with Brooklyn's Borough

of two million plus. But our little
neighborhood basks in being small.
And now the breeze is thick with falling

whirligigs that fall as when so long ago
we walked five shady blocks to Jane
and Georgie's any given day in early June.

That's when, en route, you caught
and pasted them to my shirt and face
for the first time. Little did we know

such kids' games crossed the sea
with smallpox, syphilis, and lynching.
Time's dichotomous gravity holds back

what it projects. Creates as it destroys.
Atrophy and entropy. Old age
and youth. The head and tails of life.

Our conversation goes along these lines:
There was no violence. And no gentrifying.
Now, there's both. The boy who drowned

under ice as others skated past, oblivious.
A headless cat found in the trash.
The fires lit in vacant lots. The illicit

dope and fireworks that passed
behind the Raceway, and the rest.
"Never take smokes from a stranger,"

he exhorted. Such dangers lurked.
By now, you think you would know
what to do about important things.

How to live. How to die. How to love.
By now, too much has weighed things down
for us, dragging someone else along to ease

the guilt. But it's one you're glad to dance
with. Talk to. We can only speak of happy times,
too scared to think about alone.

"Sunny days, the same sunny days,"
I murmur to myself a little sadly as I leave
your gate, knowing that the great white ash

is dying where we buried turtles: Timmy,
Martha, and Sam. Online I glimpse
where they have planted trees to save the park.

"For what new burial? Trees for Israel?"
Lenny asks. Nature's code for dying
can be found in a Museum magpie beak,

a mothwing, or a tiger tooth in amber.
Or an Indian's tortoise shell mask,
in a prehistoric seed, or a prehistoric
city map, all of them so life like.

And they seem to sing to me.
Head down, I glimpse blackened gum
and dog smudge on the pave at Army Arch,

itself a work of violence and art.
The Rotary. The infant dead. Millions
of intended and the unintended dead,

they call casualties, in the never
ending cycle of so many centuries
of war, the human plague.

War survivors and objectors hiding,
cowering in remorse along with armies
of exhausted heroes. All of it today

in nature's code for dying rises up
to me from pigeon poop and car exhaust.
I hear it on the subway

and in talk-show hosts' hoarse voices
screaming expletives or euphony
with tired listeners whose only hope

is for relief. It is this helplessness I hear.
The code for death is found in keepsakes.
G.I. dog tags, army fatigues, boots,

and in the memories of comrades living,
or disabled, many of whom have loved it all
and love retelling all. And those that died.

Would some of them say, "Let's do it
again!" or, "Not again!?" Would some
implore, "Not again!" if they could?

Here Lenny grabs another beer and adds,
"It's what I hear all the time
at V.A. checker tourneys!"

Or on a warm, June day when the code
for dying's here on Second Street,
where the sky seems filled with ghosts,

and on the corner there's the ghost
of an old as cellophane organ grinder
and another of his green-vested monkey

wringing hands and feet.
I once read in a speech
by Chief Seattle that the stars

all are our ancestors. Indians
the brightest ones, still keep watch
as he muses. And I think they pray

for us as much as we should pray
for them. And all the ancestors.
I find the code for dying in trash

flames where crones and winos
warming hands in winter, smoke
what they can find, noses reddened

in slurred speech, companionably
arguing about the latest news of the day.
Under a park bench sleeper

on this June afternoon, sea breezes
stir October leaves. Walt Whitman's
"Life,"—like maple whirligigs buried

beyond the parent tree, and that sprout
and spread the species—his "Life,"
I say, has left us in a world

in which dead bones will also rise
and join the dance. Lenny adds,
"Amen!" and, "Do you mean,

they rise like ghosts?" holding all
he can of sky between his hands.

VIII.

It's night. Eyes closed. And I withdraw
into dreams. Here there are no tenses.

In fog a mandrake points like a douser
and is male, is female, dousing for

I know not what with its hands or are they feet
at water's edge. Harpies fly off, rising

from the water, casting sea-chased spells
to haunt the pages of a sea-chased world,

our life's blood. And I wake being here
in thin imperfect probing inside human

agency, yet feel so like a fiddler crab,
looking out from behind my cover,

doing nothing with my periscoping eyes
but waiting silent and alone in the kelp shrouds.

I start writing. And the rolling waves
begin to speak. I listen as the mist

slowly lifts and words seem to come
to me as if from somewhere else.

Conversing through the night,
rolling in and out are waves of time
that turn future back to past.

From which we dangle, tethered to
the moment and its slipping thread.
Silent. Hold on tightly. We don't know

what's coming next. This is the center
of imagining. Were you not dead
among sad whisperers you'd be arguing,

"It's too late! Too late now! Fear
subverts you like an angler's back-lash.
Cut the line. Quick. Cut it.

Roll it up now. Hang it up! Enough!"
Had you spoken from your coffin at St. James's
when they joked and praised and never

once were mawkish, had you risen
from your coffin trenchant, and were we
quiet enough—while you quoted

Wallace Stevens playing Picasso's
blue guitar in dead pan through your new
pink exit hole—then we would have heard

the faintest echo of an interrupted serenade:
silent, sarcastic as your bitter smile!
The twanging gets complex then fades

as if on other sides of moons (away from light)
to pleasure goddesses you worshiped,
moving forward endlessly as beauty

does, and far beyond. Remember
monuments of sound that played
when they played things as they are;

that play as if the dead lived on
when played upon your blue guitar.
Remember how it happened?

When your wife the waitress
turned to ask, "what's yours tonight?"
you said, " It's death I want,"

where we all go and come from.
On the old man's blue guitar.
The not so old man that you are

is how you are when played
upon the blue guitar. Old
Wallace Stevens playing things

you loved so as they are.
And were and were not so.
And are now so and not so.

He knew this would be sad.
Listening, Lenny blows a kiss,
"You will never get it right!"

Evocation
> "The bird lies still while the light goes on flying." —W. S. Merwin [16]

Those with strapped-on wings
for ages dreamt of flying like the birds

and fell from cliffs broke limbs or died.
But when I ask for the wind's help

getting beyond the mind's bent roads
and its dead ends it sighs and says

(with a whoosh) I'll take you there
just as soon as all your words are ash.

---

[16] from "Unknown Age" by W. S. Merwin.

Autumn [17]
"Herbst," —Rainer Maria Rilke

The leaves fall, fall as from afar,
As if distant gardens wither in the *sky*;
They fall with negative reply.

And the heavy earth falls in the nights
In solitude from all the stars.

We're all falling. Falling too is this hand.
And look at the others: it is in all.

And yet there's One who holds this falling
Endlessly gently in his hands.

[17] "Herbst." Translated with help from Dr. Katrina Nousek, Visiting Assistant Professor of German Studies, University of Richmond.

Herbst

Die Blätter fallen, fallen wie von weit,
als welkten in den Himmeln ferne Gärten;
sie fallen mit verneinender Gebärde.

Und in den Nächten fällt die schwere Erde
aus allen Sternen in die Einsamkeit.

Wir alle fallen. Diese Hand da fällt.
Und sieh dir andre an: es ist in allen.

Und doch ist Einer, welcher dieses Fallen
unendlich sanft in seinen Händen hält.

—Rainer Marie Rilke

Richard Becker grew up in Brooklyn, NY. As a child, his mother regularly took him to Prospect Park and The Brooklyn Museum, exposing him to natural beauty and fine art. He studied piano and composition at Eastman School of Music, University of Texas, Austin, and Boston University.

As a poet, he has published in journals such as *Columbia, America, The Baltimore Review, U City Review, Cold Mountain Review,* among others. His chapbook, *Fates*, is published by *The Literary Review*. He has given poetry readings in Paris at Cité Internationale des Arts and Shakespeare & Co., in the US at Vermont Studio Center, BreadLoaf Writers Conference, Fredericksburg Center for the Creative Arts, University of Richmond, Hawaii University, Waikiki (2022), and numerous bookstores in the Richmond area.

As a pianist, he has performed on numerous college campuses and at venues such as New York's Tully Hall, The Town Hall, 92nd Street Y, Carnegie Hall, Coolidge Auditorium of the Library of Congress, The National Gallery of Art, and, as First Prize Laureate of the French Piano Institute, at the French Embassy in Washington, DC. In Paris, he has performed at L'École Normale de Musique's Salle Cortot and at Salle Michelet, a venue of the Cité Internationale des Arts, where he has been a frequent artist-in-residence. As a composer, he has been a MacDowell Colony Fellow, a Virginia Center for Creative Arts Fellow and an American Academy of Arts and Letters nominee.

His music compositions have been performed at Tanglewood Music Center, L'École Normale de Musique, Brattleboro Music Festival, National Gallery of Art, Virginia Museum, University of South Florida, and on college campuses throughout the country. His compositions have received Meet the Composer Grants, Contemporary Music Studio grants, and wide critical acclaim in the press. His piano performance has been described as "powerful" by the Washington Post, "admirable in taste and technique" by the New York Times, and "brilliant with seamless passagework and elegant phrasing" by the Richmond Times-Dispatch.

He lives in Richmond, VA with his wife Doris Wylee-Becker, with whom he plays two-piano concerts, their daughter Ilana Lee, and Golden Retriever Muffin. He is Associate Professor of Music at the University of Richmond, where he heads Piano Study, teaches piano and a course called "Poetry and Music."

www.ingramcontent.com/pod-product-compliance
Lightning Source LLC
LaVergne TN
LVHW041556070426
835507LV00011B/1119